GET READY FOR A WORLD OF ACTION AND ADVENTURE!

Check it out, spider fans! There's a new villain in town and he goes by the name of Dr Octopus. I gotta stop this psycho-squid before he wrecks the city, so grab your web-spinners and get ready for some serious arachnid action!

IS THIS THE END OF SPIDER-MAN?! WILL HIS TRUE IDENTITY BE REVEALED BY THE STRANGEST FOE OF ALL TIME?

BITTEN BY AN IRRADIATED SPIDER, WHICH GRANTED HIM INCREDIBLE ABILITIES, **PETER PARKER** LEARNED THE ALL-IMPORTANT LESSON, THAT WITH GREAT POWER THERE MUST ALSO COME GREAT RESPONSIBILITY. AND SO HE BECAME THE AMAZING...

SPIDER-MAN versus DOCTOR OCTOPUS

STAN LEE & STEVE DITKO	DANIEL QUANTZ	MARK BROOKS	DANIMATION with SIMON YEUNG	ERIK KO	VC'S RANDY GENTILE
PLOT	SCRIPT	ARTIST	COLORS	UDON CHIEF	LETTERER

MACKENZIE CADENHEAD & NICK LOWE	C.B. CEBULSKI	RALPH MACCHIO	JOE QUESADA	DAN BUCKLEY
ASSISTANT EDITORS	EDITOR	CONSULTING EDITOR	EDITOR-IN-CHIEF	PUBLISHER

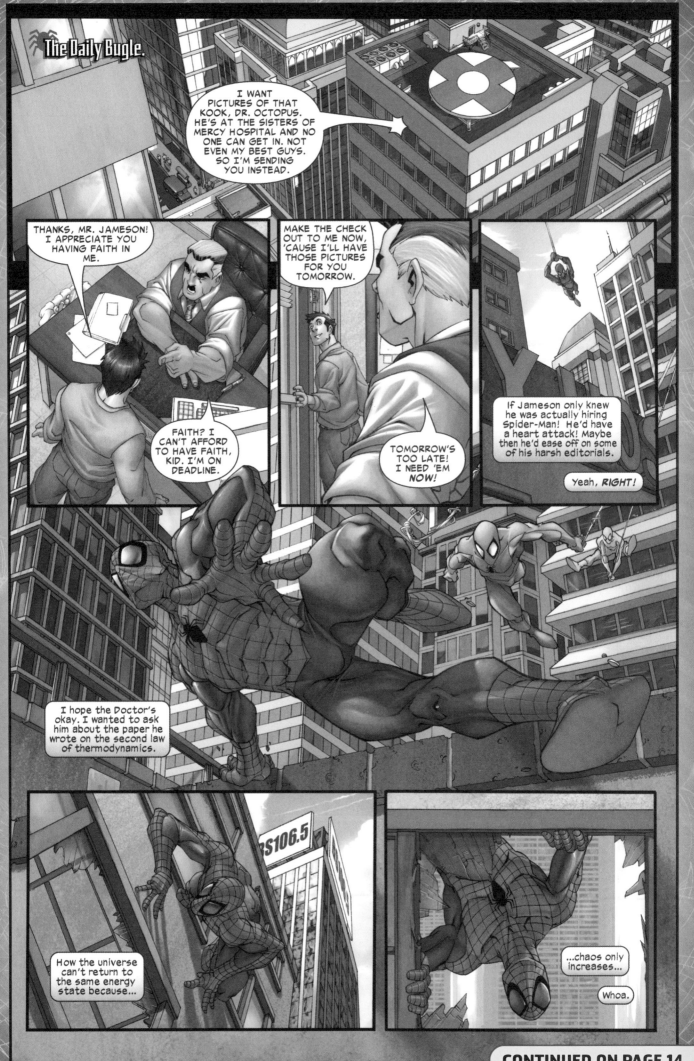

CONTINUED ON PAGE 14

SPIDEY CENTRAL!

Those crazy mechanical arms are going to make fighting Doc Ock a real challenge. I'm gonna need a hand for this scrap, so help me out by answering these puzzles!

CAMERA OBSCURED!

Doc Ock's tentacles have wrecked Pete's camera and ruined all his recent photos! Can you tell who is in each of the pictures he has taken?

A

B

E

C

D

MULTIPLE MENACE!

Take a look at these five pictures of Dr Octopus and see if you can tell which one matches the original!

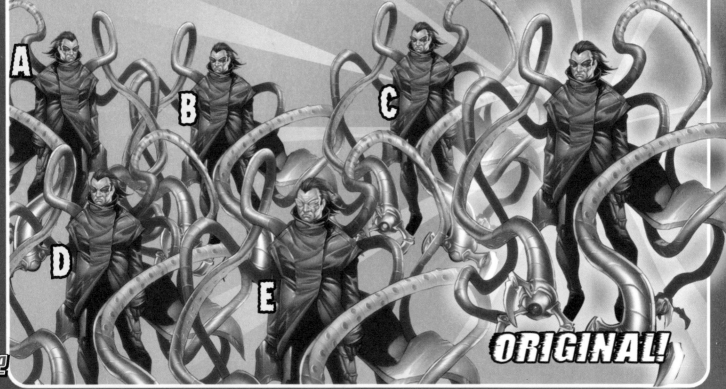

A

B

C

D

E

ORIGINAL!

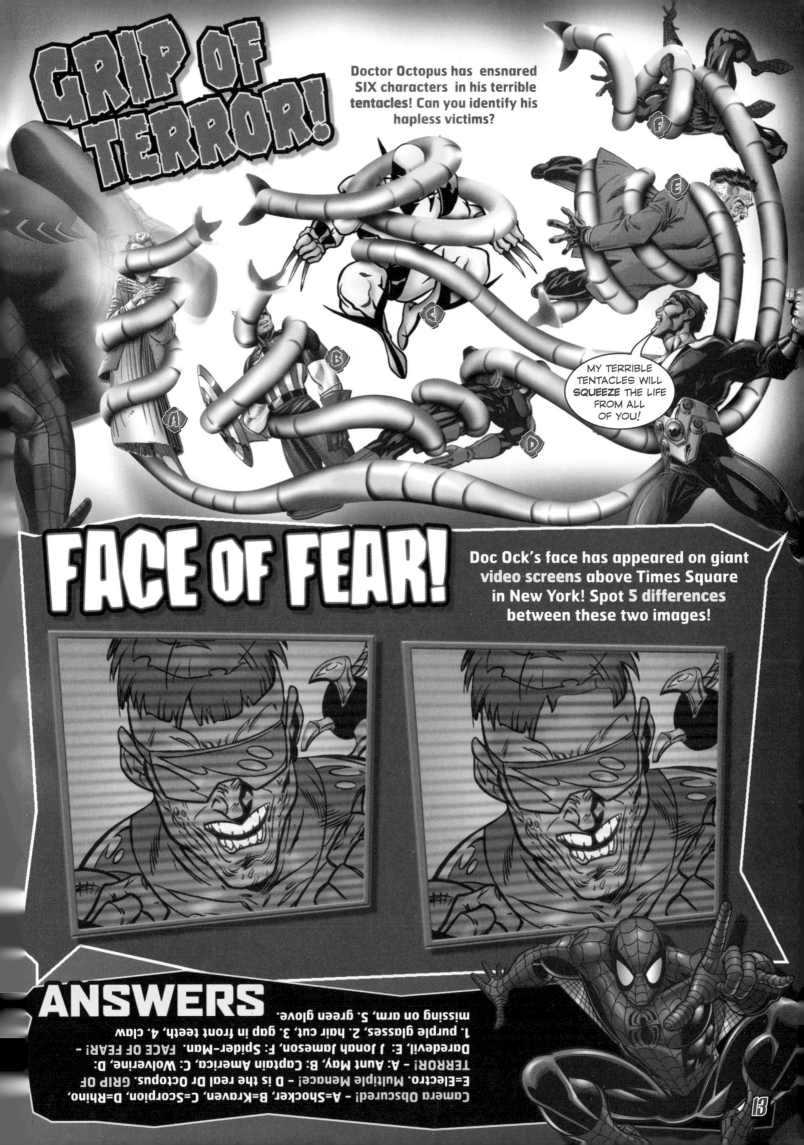

GRIP OF TERROR!

Doctor Octopus has ensnared SIX characters in his terrible tentacles! Can you identify his hapless victims?

MY TERRIBLE TENTACLES WILL SQUEEZE THE LIFE FROM ALL OF YOU!

FACE OF FEAR!

Doc Ock's face has appeared on giant video screens above Times Square in New York! Spot 5 differences between these two images!

ANSWERS

Camera Obscured! - A=Shocker, B=Kraven, C=Scorpion, D=Rhino, E=Electro. Multiple Menace! - D is the real Dr Octopus. GRIP OF TERROR! - A: Aunt May, B: Captain America, C: Wolverine, D: Daredevil, E: J Jonah Jameson, F: Spider-Man. FACE OF FEAR! - 1. purple glasses, 2. hair cut, 3. gap in front teeth, 4. claw missing on arm, 5. green glove.

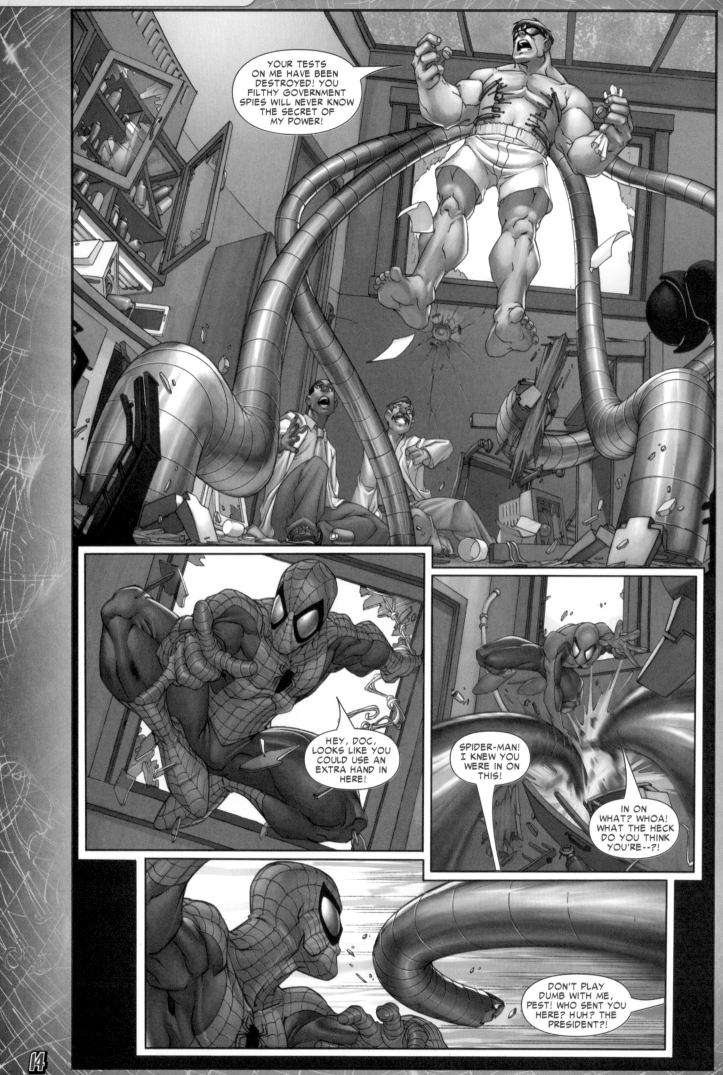

DOCTOR OCTOPUS

Even the bravest heroes think twice before going toe-to-toe (or should that be toe-to-tentacle?) with the dreaded Doc Ock! Read on to find out all about him!

REAL NAME: DR OTTO OCTAVIUS
OCCUPATION: CRIMINAL MASTERMIND
HEIGHT: 5' 9"
WEIGHT: 245 LBS
EYE COLOUR: BROWN
HAIR COLOUR: BROWN
BASE OF OPERATIONS: NEW YORK AREA
POWERS / ABILITIES: HIS BODY IS FUSED TO FOUR INCREDIBLY STRONG METAL TENTACLES, WHICH OBEY HIS EVERY COMMAND!
QUOTE:
"IGNORANT WHELP! NO MAN CAN MATCH THE GENIUS OF DR OTTO OCTAVIUS!"

STRENGTH:

AGILITY:

INTELLIGENCE:

SPEED:

FIGHTING SKILL:

First Appearance:
The Amazing
Spider-Man #3
(1963)

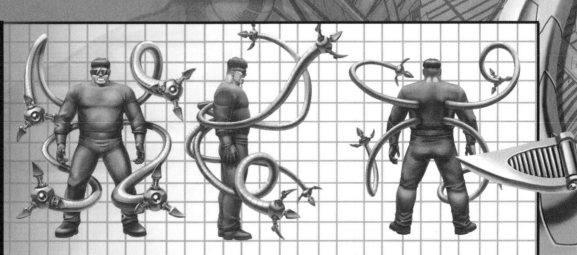

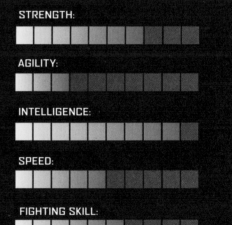

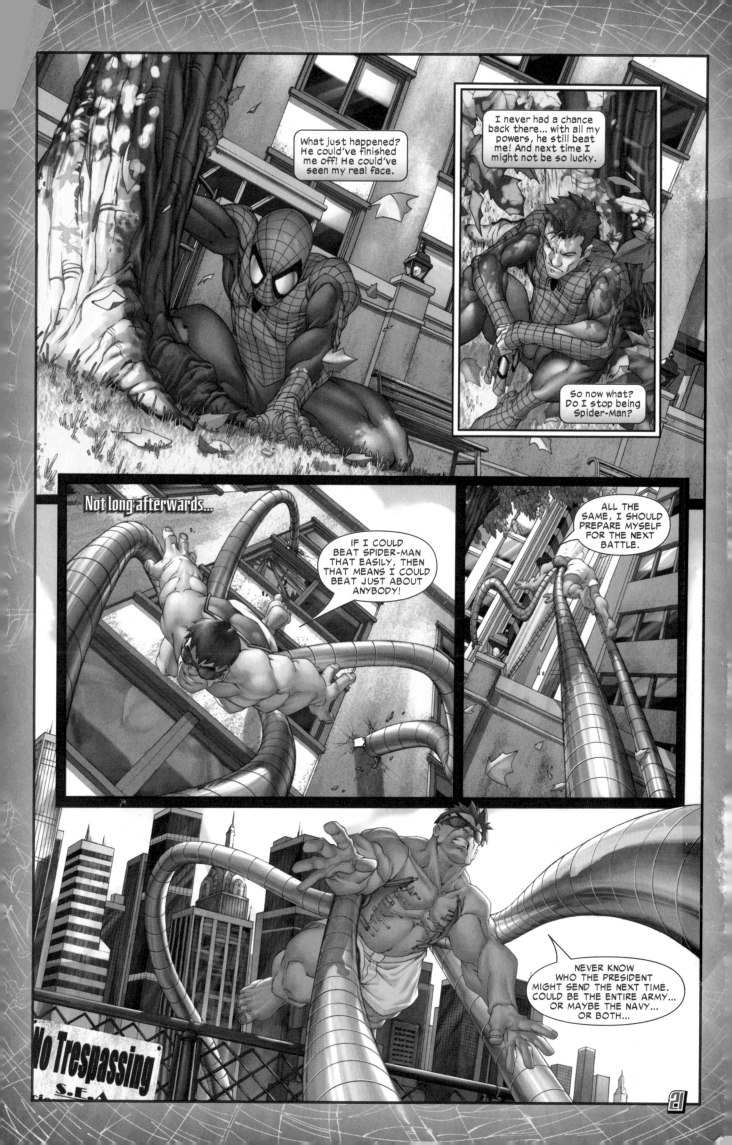

TENTACLE TRAVEL!

Doc Ock can run on his tentacles at a top speed of **50 mph**. He can also use them as springs to propel himself up to **100 feet** into the air.

ARMED COMBAT!

The level of control he has over his tentacles is so precise he can fight **multiple opponents** at once, sometimes with each limb fighting a **different person**!

KNOCKOUT BLOW!

Despite their size, each mechanical arm can move at a *lightning fast* speed of **90 feet per second**, and can deliver a blow strong enough to knock even Spidey off his feet.

THWACK!

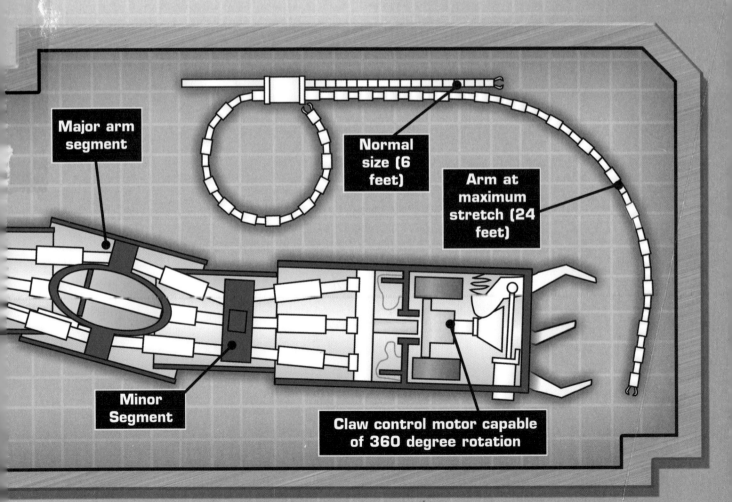

Major arm segment

Normal size (6 feet)

Arm at maximum stretch (24 feet)

Minor Segment

Claw control motor capable of 360 degree rotation

HELPING HANDS!

Dr Otto Octavius was a brilliant scientist and one of the world's leading experts in **atomic energy**. He created an incredible set of **mechanical arms** designed to keep him safe whilst performing *highly dangerous* experiments. These extra limbs earned him the nickname '**Dr Octopus**' amongst his co-workers.

DISASTER STRIKES!

But the *peaceful scientist* was forever changed when one of his experiments went disastrously wrong and **exploded** in front of him. The blast was so intense it *fused* his delicate **mechanical harness** directly to his body.

A CHANGED MAN!

Now able to control his tentacles through a strange *psychic bond,* Otto realised that he could use his new powers and genius intellect to take whatever he wanted. Turning his back on science he created a new destiny for himself as the *twisted* criminal mastermind **Dr Octopus!**

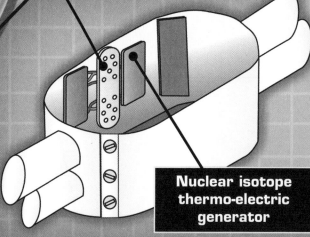

TENTACLE TECHNOLOGY!

Want to know how Doc Ock's mechanical arms work? We've managed to track down a secret blueprint that reveals the secrets of his terrible tentacles.

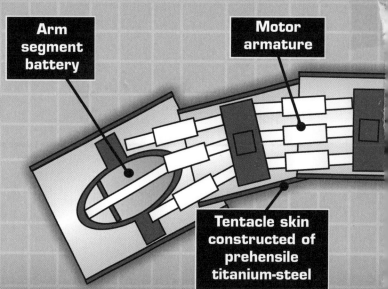

Spinal tap nerve impulse inducers

Arm segment battery

Motor armature

Nuclear isotope thermo-electric generator

Tentacle skin constructed of prehensile titanium-steel

TEN THINGS YOU NEVER KNEW ABOUT... DOCTOR OCTOPUS!

Doctor Octopus has been a thorn in Spidey's side since the very beginning of his crime-fighting career! Read on to discover TEN amazing facts about the demented Doctor!

> OF COURSE I REMEMBER YOU! YOU'RE THAT KINDLY DR. OCTOPUS WHOM I VISITED IN 1964 WITH MISS BETTY BRANT!*

> NOW THAT I REALIZE YOU ARE TO BE THE LANDLADY, DEAR MRS. PARKER, I WILL ACCEPT THE ROOM SIGHT UNSEEN!

> AND TO THINK IT'S YOU WHO ARE ANSWERING OUR AD FOR A BOARDER!

> WHAT A SMALL WORLD!

1 TENTACLED TENANT!

Otto Octavius once rented a room in Aunt May's house. All the time he was there, she never realised that he was an escaped criminal!

2 IMPRESSIVE REACH!

Even though his tentacles appear to be only six feet long, they can extend to over twenty-five feet!

3 WEDDING BELLS!

We never thought Dr. Octopus was much of a ladies-man, but it turns out that he once very nearly married Aunt May! Luckily Spider-Man saved his beloved Aunt from Doc Ock's clutches!

4 OCTO-IMPOSTER!

A man known only as Mr. Carlyle once kidnapped Doc Ock and managed to recreate his own version of the Doctor's trademark tentacles. Thankfully Spidey successfully put an end to his unlawful antics!

5 DOC, OCK JUNIOR!

A young boy called Ollie Osnick greatly admired Dr. Octopus and built his own set of tentacles so he could team up with his hero against Spider-Man!

6 NON-STICK NUISANCE!

His four tentacles are coated in a special substance that makes it impossible for Spider-Man to stick his webs to them!

7 ANOTHER OCTOPUS!

Ollie Osnick wasn't the only person to copy Doc Ock! Whilst he was in prison, a brilliant scientist called Carolyn Trainer acquired his tentacles and used them for her own plans. However, as soon as Doc Ock had escaped from prison, she willingly gave them back to him.

8 A QUIET CHILD...

Much like Peter Parker, Dr. Octopus was very shy and quiet as a child. He much preferred staying inside and studying to being outside playing with friends.

9 MEMORY BLOCK!

Whilst suffering from a bad case of amnesia, Spider-Man was tricked into working for Dr. Octopus! However, it didn't take Spidey long to realise that even though he couldn't remember anything, he knew that Dr. Octopus was not the kind of person he wanted to be mixed up with!

10 and finally...

As crazy as it sounds, Dr. Octopus has four mechanical tentacles attached to his body that he can control with the power of his mind! (Actually, I'm guessing you guys probably noticed that one already...)

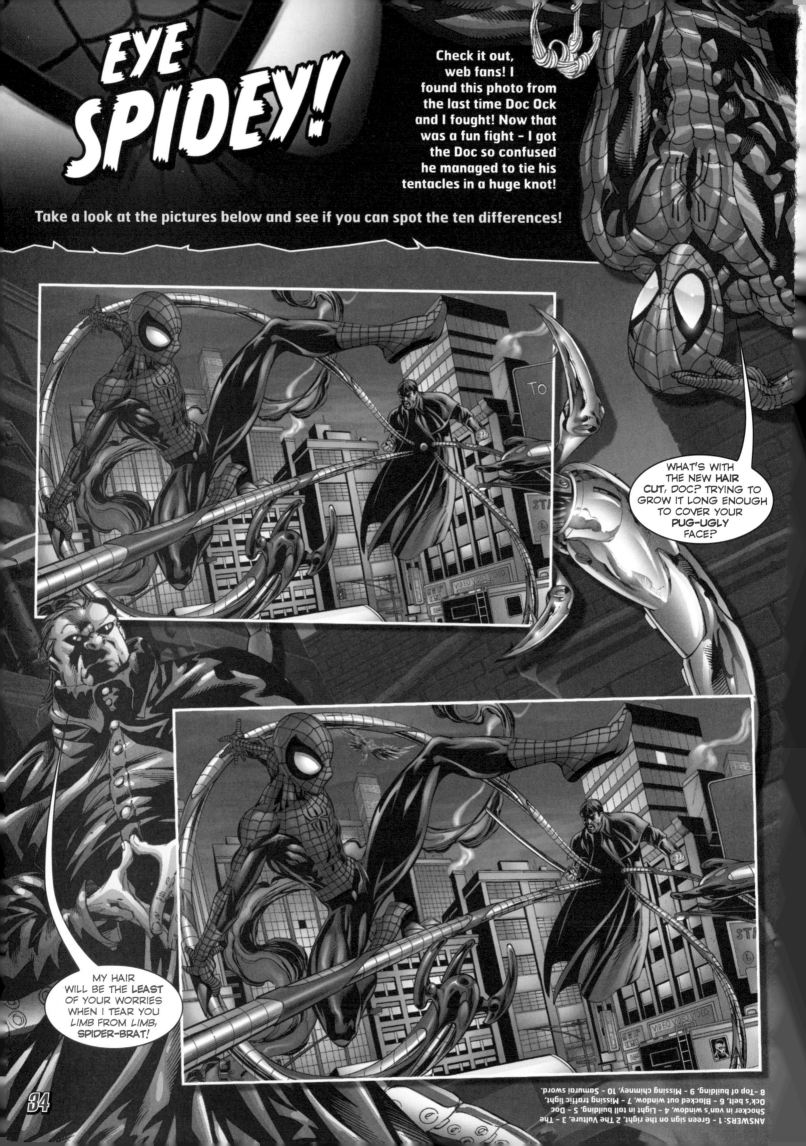